Am I Even HUMAN?

TC Ranae

Presentation by *BookLeaf Publishing*

Web: www.bookleafpub.com

E-mail: info@bookleafpub.com

ISBN: 978-93-5744-491-0

First edition 2022

This book is dedicated to anyone who has ever questioned their own feelings. Your feelings are real and they are valid. Never forget that.

ACKNOWLEDGEMENT

Quick "thank you" to the following:

My family for always being supportive of whatever I want to accomplish.

My boyfriend for staying up with me during all the late nights.

My friends for always being available to bounce ideas off.

Glen Retief and Dr. Krystal Berry Curtis for always believing in me.

All the writers before me that showed me this was possible.

Kind of Lover

The pain is real.
Filled with unseen bruises and crusted tears.
It can't be mistaken that this pain is real.
Unseen but real.
Depression is a ruthless thing
Almost like a toxic lover.
You know you don't want it
You know it's no good for you, but you can't get
rid of it for the life of you.
It is an "Until death do us part" kind of lover.
An "I won't hurt you again" kind of lover.
A "You took that the wrong way, so suck it up"
kind of lover.
A "You're nothing without me" kind of lover.
A "You're better off dead" kind of lover.
Broken promises, forgotten words and sad songs
that only teach you
That your kind of lover
Might be right.

C & L

Clouded thoughts
Cracked lips
And crimson eyes
Long nights
Lowlights
And lethal cries
Never ending days
That whisper your name
Into the abyss
Of unfinished dreams
That gleam with the tears
Of a child that was lost
And still has not been found

Pieces

The windows to my soul are broken
Destroyed by misguided words and forever
scathed images
That can never be erased
Your words linger against my skin
Like butterfly wings in the Summer breeze
And at the same time
Like frozen tears against my cheek
This pain is undying
Breathing
Waiting
To swallow me whole
However
Lucky me
I am in

Pieces.

O.D.

White lines

Of promised silence
And forgotten memories
The aching in my chest
Tapping against my body
Like the tiny
Blade
Against the table
Creating both separation
And perfection
A dollar bill tunnel

To Euphoria

A silent kiss
To darkened Peace

Forever.

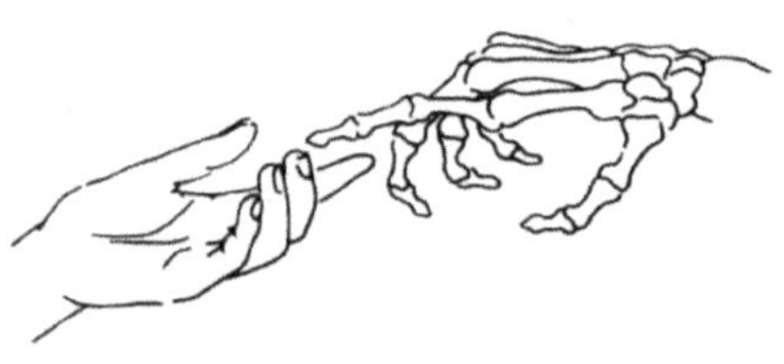

In this one bed
It holds two bodies
So close
Yet so distant
Oceans and dreams
Stardust and time
Pass between the void
That is our connection
A boy cries
-         for lost love
A girl aches
-         for stolen peace

Fragile beings
Become
Fragile minds
Broken bones
Hurt less than
The broken heart
Wrapped in
Anxiety and Misunderstandings
Depression and Fear
This one bed
Holds
No one.

HOUSE

I am a House
I am a House with stories and hidden
complexities
My exterior is inviting
But my interior is cold
Filled with broken promises and forgotten words
Mirrors are filled with spider web cracks and
glasses are shattered beyond repair
Hanging on the walls are the remains of love
notes that never made it; lost and forgotten
No longer starting from who but only to whom
You say we buy "Ugly Houses" but why not me?
Am I not good enough?
Did I not reach your standards?
I am falling apart
Crawling with an infestation of emotions that
don't make sense
Because I am a House
Who just wants to be a Home

Kind of Lover II

You
Are the kind of lover
My brain wants
And my heart needs
The kind of lover
That reminds my heart that love is real
My feelings are real
That the endless storm of emotions
In my soul
Are real
But are not wrong
That I am valid
My bruises are valid
And that what I feel for you
Is
Valid.

Drown

The air is murky
As I breathe the solidness of it in my lungs
My eyes burn
Against the immediate pressure to shine
I can't breathe
And I drown in front of your eyes
With a smile on my lying lips
And tears pouring from my broken soul

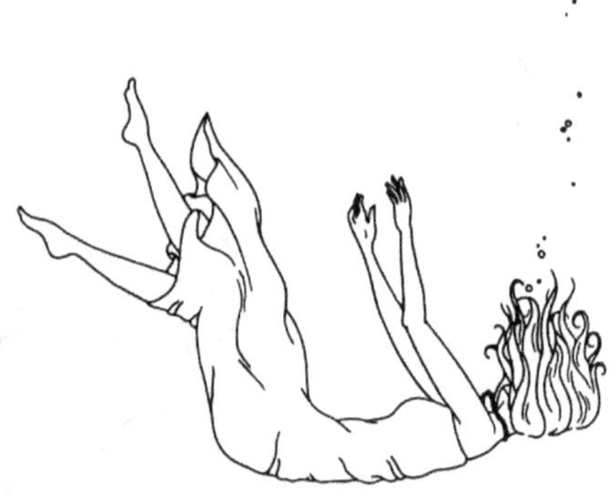

Just Right

You speak to me in ways
That no one else could ever understand
Butterfly Laughs
And
Fingertip Kisses
Intimacy without being Intimate
Our Love Language filled hearts
Playing telephone
As if they were children
Meeting up again
And maybe they are
Because with you
The world doesn't feel Dark or overly Bright
With you
My heart doesn't have to be too hard or too soft
With you
Everything
Is just right

There was something in loving you
That reminded me
That everything would be okay
That storms
Were still clouds
That dark places
Only needed flashlights
That dusk
Always turned into dawn
And that hues of blue
Were not always sad
That sometimes the blues
Could be endless skies of love
Falling into their forever
Of everlasting
Light.

Remind me

The sweet smell
Of Oak
lilies
Will always remind me
Of Summer Nights
winter Mornings
While the empty ghost
That is your presence
Will remind me
Of Broken Promises
scorching Cries

1 cup of Broken Heart
3 cloves of Clouded mind
A dash of Lost
& A sprinkle of Time
2 teaspoons of Sorrow filled Tears
¼ cup of Pride
2 tablespoons of Love
& 2 scoops of Lies
A recipe for Disaster
Addictive in taste
But bitter to the soul

Senses

Your stare was the first song I ever sung,
Innocent and Alluring,
But now I've lost my voice and I'm scared

Your smell was the first spark of an open flame,
Warm and Resonating,
But now the fire has died and I'm alone.

Your voice was the first home in my heart, built
from Ashes and Patience,
But now it's haunted and I'm dying

Your touch was the first sip of white wine,
Delicious and always left me wanting more,
But now the bottle is empty and I'm a Lush

Your smile was the first breeze of Spring,
Gentle and Inviting,
But now it's storming and I'm freezing

My problems
Begin and End
With you
And I'm certain
I may too

Let me hold
Your gentle heart
In the palms of my hands
As we close our eyes
And breathe in the sweet silence
That is our space
Showered in
Patience
And protected in
Peace

Let me

The spaces between my fingers
Are yours to hold
Missing puzzle pieces
Create the final picture
That our hearts are desperate
To complete
Let me
Drink from your lips my name
And in return
Let my soul feed yours
Filling the darkness
You desperately hide
Let me
Kiss the river that drenches your face while you
sleep
And drowns your heart in sorrow
Let me
Be the shelter your mind searches for
To love
And be Loved.

Darkness
Is what laid between her eyes
Polishing the songs of never-ending cries
Darkness
Was the cloak around her heart
Suffocating and silently ripping it apart
Darkness was forever
But so was her hope
That her Darkness
Would be lit up with Stars

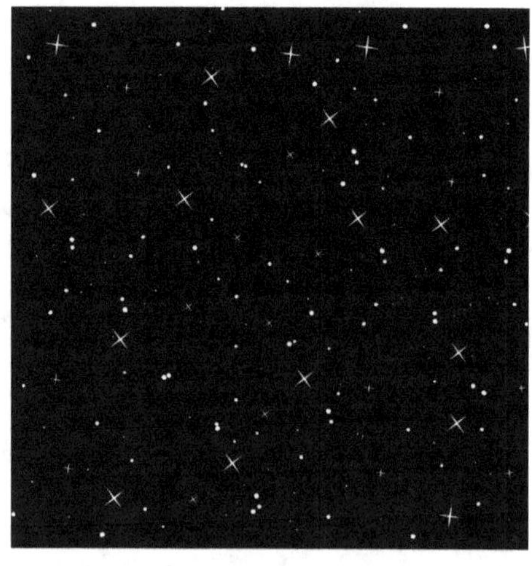

My Ode to You

On nights like these
Where I am wide awake
Right next to your resting form
I sit and wonder
How someone like you
Looked at someone like me and thought
I will teach them the beauty in love
How light rains are tiny kisses
And sunrises are hello
That windy days are my caresses
And that goodbyes don't exist in true love
That even when apart
You remain in the heart
That true love is more than words can explain
Our love is more than words can explain
Oh, how did I
Get so lucky?

My.

I do not remember my first kiss
Or hello
I do not remember my first spark
Or laugh
Whenever I think about
What might have been my first
Pictures of you are what swarm my head
Invade my thoughts
Brighten my cheeks
And sweat my palms
You may not be my first
But my body so desperately wants you
To be my last

Poet

There is something in writing poetry
Something in knowing that
As my fingers tap against the keys
My emotions speak
In a way I can't
Something in knowing that
The person who reads this
May understand me better
And know what it feels like
To be awake in the middle of the night
Looking at a screen
Hoping it will write the words
That are locked in a room
But has no key
Words that beg to be heard
But have no mouth, no voice
No outlet
And are left
Feeling
Empty…

Believing in something without proof is hard.
Evidence is vital yet we're expected to believe
in something we cannot see.
Karma.
God.
Fate.
A narrow path of wonder
Longing for answers
Yet at the sight of you
I knew all three were true
Only Karma would allow my rightful acts to
finally be recognized
Only God would force me to fight through
darkness to find Light
And only Fate would bring me to you.
Karma whispers in my ear good job
God whispers flashlight
And Fate whispers journey
Two lives becoming One path
Spelling forever.

Inner War

Frigid waters
Heavy breaths
Silent screams
Burning eyes
The waves crash against the rigid shore
Thrashing for freedom
Release

Sweet girl
Drowning in Daylight
Cold lips
Split into a grin
Gatekeeper teeth
Hold secrets
And an aching soul

Grasping hands
In pitted Darkness
Shred the Soul
Her No
Accepted as Yes
Her Silence
The Greenlight to Continue

Bladed grass
Cool breeze
Angel kisses

Fairy wings
Prayers are answered for Peace
Sufferable silence heard
A fresh breath fills the air

Sweet girl
Floats in Daylight
Fluttered eyes
New Mornings
Bring new Beginnings
The soul shines
The heart beating once again.